12 WAYS
TO DEVELOP
A POSITIVE ATTITUDE

12 Ways to Develop a Positive Attitude

◦ ◦ ◦

A Tyndale Treasure by
DALE E. GALLOWAY

Tyndale House
Publishers, Inc.
Wheaton, Illinois

Twelve Ways to Develop a Positive Attitude
is adapted from *Dream a New Dream*
by Dale E. Galloway,
copyright © 1975 by
Tyndale House Publishers, Inc.,
Wheaton, Illinois.

Library of Congress Catalog Card Number 75-39809
ISBN 0-8423-7550-3
Printed in the United States of America.

97   96   95   94
28   27   26   25

ACCEPT WHAT
YOU CANNOT CHANGE

The church sanctuary was beautifully decorated with mistletoe and holly, and a huge Christmas tree covered with gorgeous ornaments and twinkling lights stood in the corner. It was Christmas Sunday, 1970. From all over Portland our growing congregation had come together to celebrate the joyful occasion of our Lord's birth. If there was ever a man who loves to preach, it is me, and Christmas Sunday is one of my favorite Sundays of the year. Normally I would be at my best for a big Sunday like Christmas. In years to come I would look back on that Sunday morning, not remembering what I said, and wonder how I ever stood up, faced the people, and proclaimed the joys of Christmas on the saddest day of my life.

It all happened exactly as my wife had told me months before that it would. According to her pre-planned time schedule, a total stranger handed me those dreadful divorce papers on that fateful Friday a few days before Christmas. Within twenty-four hours I stood at the Portland International Airport, and through misty eyes watched helplessly as the woman I had loved, honored, and cherished since I was eighteen years old led my two children onto an airplane and departed, never to return. Many times as a minister I have heard people talk like they thought there were some things worse than death. At that moment and in the following days, for me, life was worse than death.

What would I do? In less than twenty-four hours I was expected to preach the Christmas message to my congregation. I recalled a wonderful friend of mine whom I had admired when I was growing up and who I thought was a beautiful minister for God. Into his life came one of these shattering experiences. Ironically, it was just a couple of days before Christmas Sunday. Instead of standing up to the situation, he ran for dear life. He phoned my dad, who was the church administrator, late on Saturday night and told him that he was held up in a motel and wouldn't be at the church on Christmas Sunday. I remembered, as a young man, thinking what a shock that would be for the congregation, to come and find that their leader had, under pressure, fled the scene. Now I understood why he ran. At this time, I felt like running away and never coming back.

Several months before I had any knowledge of my impending, heartbreaking split-up, I had preached a sermon to my congregation, centering on the Prayer of Serenity. I shared with them how on many occasions in counseling, I had pointed people to this beautiful prayer, and that when people practiced it in their lives, it brought peace to their struggles. Little did I know how much I would soon desperately need this Prayer of Serenity:

2

God grant me the serenity
to accept the things I cannot change . . .
courage to change the things I can . . .
and wisdom to know the difference.

Stand up and face the music. I would have given anything in my power to avoid, to alter, to delay, to just stop that terrible day from coming. No one likes to hang out their dirty linen for the world to see, let alone a person who has been brought up to believe that the ministry should be far above the sins of humanity. I guess I would have been willing to have stayed home more nights, instead of spending so much of my time and energy away from home working with other people. I would have promised and tried to carry out anything she wanted if I could only have changed the nightmarish reality of that fateful day. I would have been willing to take all the blame. I was beginning to learn the first part of an important truth. There are some things that, try as you may, you cannot change. Whatever I might have done to avoid that moment was forever gone.

At the close of my sermon on that unforgettable Christmas Sunday, emotionally choked up and with difficulty, I announced to the congregation that I would like to meet them for a congregational meeting in the Fellowship Hall immediately following the service. The people jammed into the Fellowship Hall to see what the big deal was. I took a deep breath, stepped forward, and with God's help faced the music. I stated that my wife had chosen to leave, had filed for divorce, had taken the two children, and planned never to return. I asked them for forgiveness for my failure as a husband and

3

to please pray for both parties at this time. People stood there in shock, not knowing what to say. I opened the floor up for questions, but, thank God, there weren't any.

Don't run from the things you can't change. Stand up to them. A man becomes bigger than the thing he stands up to.

In the days ahead, I was to learn many more lessons about what I could not change. *There are things that cannot be changed, no matter how hard you struggle*. A few days later I stood at the bedside of a twenty-four-year-old, extremely intelligent woman who wanted so much to live and had everything to live for. Her ambition was to become a great trial lawyer, and she had the ability to achieve that goal. But now her body was stricken by a fatal disease. As we visited one day toward the end, she shared with me all her feelings concerning her fast-approaching death. She told how friends she tried to talk to would turn her off because they didn't want to talk about death. Detail by detail, she told me about the great struggle she had fought, how she felt cheated when the doctor said she would not live. She talked about all the things she wanted to do—to marry, to become a trial lawyer, to have children, to go places, do things, see things, and she told me how she had feared dying. I couldn't help but notice there was a serenity in her weakened voice. Finally, I asked her what the secret of her peace was. She will never know what she did for me when she shared that secret. Unknown to my friend, I was one of those confused strugglers. She said: "I have been at peace since that moment a few days ago when I accepted my coming death and placed myself in God's hands."

The key to peace, inside, is to accept what you cannot change and leave it in Someone's hands who is bigger than you are.

Many times I have watched people face through acceptance what looked to me to be impossible. "He is dead; I cannot bring him back." "She has left me; I cannot make her come back." Emotional healing begins as you take this first big step: Accept what you cannot change.

What we accept we not only live with, but overcome.

Recently I counseled a young woman whose husband had left her some time ago for another woman, with no desire to ever return, under any circumstances. Her doctor has tried to get her to accept this; friends have tried to get her to accept it. She refused to accept it. Consequently, she continues to be a broken, hurting person who cannot heal up.

Let's face it. There are some things you cannot change:
You cannot change the weather.
You cannot change the tick of the clock.
You cannot change the past.
You cannot change another person against his or her will.
You cannot change what is right and what is wrong.
You cannot change the march toward death on which a fatal disease takes the human body.

You cannot change the fact that a loved one has died.

Get smart. Save energy. Stop the struggle. Simply accept what you cannot change.

Accepting means that you stop fighting the inevitable. When those divorce papers were handed to me, there was a fight in me that wanted to go to court and contest the divorce for all I was worth. However, as the days passed, I began to ask myself some very important questions concerning how going to court and fighting would change anything or anyone's mind. I came to the conclusion that one cannot force another person to do something they do not choose to do. To openly fight it out in court would only compound the hurt. At this point, I asked God to help me to accept what I could not change. It was at this point of *acceptance* that my own emotional healing began. It was my first big step back from heartbreak.

I can change no other person by direct action. But when I change my attitudes and actions, people tend to change theirs in response to my change.

Acceptance stops a lot of hurt. The most difficult thing I have ever done in my life was to come to the point of surrendering the right to be with my two children, to guide their lives, to enjoy watching them grow up, to have anything at all to say in their affairs. I decided very early in the divorce proceedings that no matter how it tore me apart or what it did to me emotionally, first of all I had to discipline myself not to do anything or say anything that would tear the children apart any more emotionally. I made myself a promise that under no circumstances would I say anything derogatory about the children's mother. Acceptance for me meant she would have the children in Ohio, and because of distance I would go months, sometimes years, without seeing my children face to face. After all these years I still have an ache inside when I think about being separated from Brian and Lynette. Yet, as I continue to accept this fact, they will live with their mother and I have no more right to them—responsibility, yes, but rights, no. My complete healing at this point is taking place.

On a Saturday, I drove over a hundred miles to Centralia, Washington, to visit a dear friend who is exactly my age. John Wright was my associate pastor for several years and just a prince of a Christian and a loving worker in the Lord's work. As much as he wanted to see his two children grow up, as much as he wanted to carry on a full life of ministry to accomplish things for Jesus Christ, he had to come to accept his impending death. Courageously, with great faith, and with expectation, he now awaited death, knowing that in God's plan, the best for him was yet to come. Three days after our visit together, my friend went to Heaven.

As I left after that last visit with John, his wife and I walked out into the front yard together. We talked about the Prayer of Serenity and Faye said, "For me, acceptance takes the struggle away." Whatever it is that you face, that you can't change —give it to God. Stop struggling! The beautiful thing is that once we stop struggling, the confusion

7

is all gone, the turmoil is over, and there is peace. The peace which passes understanding, which God gives generously to all those who accept what they cannot change. Accept. Then you, too, can have peace in the midst of the storm.

Never worry about anything that is out of your power to change. About ninety-five percent of what we worry and stew about are little things that we cannot change. When I first started our drive-in church ministry, I would worry every weekend about what the weather was going to be like. Was it going to rain? Was the sun going to shine? Unfortunately, or fortunately depending on which way you view it, it rains many weekends here in Oregon. Then I talked to Dr. Robert Schuller, pastor of a famous walk-in/drive-in church (Garden Grove Community Church) in southern California, and he gave me this wisdom: "Dale, if you are going to pastor a drive-in church, don't ever worry about the weather, because you can't change it. It's in God's hands." From that day to this, I have left the weather in God's hands. Whether it rains or shines doesn't make any difference to me. I have a great Sunday every Sunday.

Stop worrying over what you cannot change and enjoy living more!

There is no gain without pain. [1] Out of my pain and agony came some needed changes in my personality. Shaken to my foundation by divorce, my eyes were opened to some things about myself that I didn't

[1] Robert Schuller, *You Can Become the Person You Want to Be* (New York: Hawthorn Books, Inc., 1973), p. 97.

like. Speeding down the road to success in hot pursuit of my goals, I had not taken the time to be aware of everyday life, to enjoy the little things that make life fun. I was too busy *doing*, to *be*. People who knew me before and who know me now testify that out of my personal tragedy came changes for the better in my personality; now I am more fun to live with and life is so much more fun to live! Before, I did not have close friends. Now I enjoy many exceptionally close friendships.

I know people can change because I, for one, am not the person I was yesterday. And with God's help I am going to keep improving and be an even better person tomorrow.

Stop trying to change that other person, and with God's help, change yourself. You, too, can change:
You can change your attitude.
You can change your personality.
You can change bad habits into good ones.
You can change your job.
You can change your marriage before it's too late.
You can change your brokenness into wholeness.

Every day people are changing, with God's help, into the beautiful people God created them to become.

Created for something greater than brokenness—that's you!

How does one know the difference between what he can change and what he cannot? By communicating with God through prayer. From childhood I was taught to sing, "What a friend we have in Jesus."

"Oh, what peace we often forfeit,
Oh, what needless pain we bear,
All because we do not carry,
Everything to God in prayer."—Joseph Scriven

Commit—David says, "Commit thy way unto the Lord; trust also in him, and he shall bring it to pass" (Psalm 37:5). This big word *commit*, when practiced completely, gives one the wisdom to know what to change and what to accept.

The commit prayer goes beyond "You take it" to "I release it." There is quite a difference. It is the prayer I made that day, driving to Bend when I entered into a new level of Spirit-filled living.

In the early months of 1971, awaiting final court action on the divorce, I found that things that had never bothered me before were worrying me to death. And I was worried about the local church, and the effect my divorce was having on the congregation.

The date arrived for me to attend the State Ministers' Conference for our denomination, to be held in Bend, Oregon. The very thought of going and having to face my fellow pastors filled me with acute anxiety. I just knew I would be the subject of their conversations. That day, as the car was heading toward Bend, I practiced what I call "Let go and let God." I took my hands and cupped them in front of me, held them up, and verbally put inside those hands everything I was fretting over and didn't have any answers to. I said out loud as I held up both hands, "There it is, God; I can't change it, I don't know what to do with it, it's all so unacceptable to me. I have been struggling over it. I

10

have been fighting it. I just don't know what to do. There it is, Lord, I give it all to you. I give to you what people think about me. I give to you what's going to happen to the local church. I give to you what's going to happen to my ministry." As I talked to God, I turned my hands upside down and said, "There it is, Lord. It's all yours." As I stretched my fingers out as far as I could, turning my hands upside down so that it was impossible to hold onto anything, as I dropped my arms to my side, a wonderful feeling of serenity suddenly spread throughout my entire being. I now had peace in the midst of the storm.

Let go and let God. Then you will know what to leave alone and what to change, and the result will be inner serenity.

MAKE THE WONDERFUL
DISCOVERY OF WHO YOU ARE

I want you to discover, as I have, what a wonderful person you really are and can become, no matter what has happened in your life, no matter what you have done or failed to do or how you think of yourself at this moment.

In God's sight you are not:

A wash-out.
A complete failure.
A hopeless sinner.

God says that you are worth loving—so begin now to love yourself. God's greatest creation is—you!

What a Creator God is! "The heavens declare the glory of God; and the firmament showeth his handiwork" (Psalm 19:1). Open your God-given eyes! The trademark of the Master Designer is upon everything in our universe. No wonder the songwriter declares of God, "How Great Thou Art"!

Of all God's wondrous creations you are his greatest! The finest; the most wonderful; the choicest; the *best!* God has made you "a little lower than the angels, and hast crowned (you) with glory and honor." He made you "to have dominion over the works of (his) hands" (Psalm 8:5, 6).

13

A divine original—that's you.

Someone special—that's you. God made you unique. There is no one else just like you. In the master planning of God himself, every man is created with many things in common. Yet each is distinct, and different from any other human being. No two snowflakes are identical. Each blade of grass is different from all others. How much greater are you than a snowflake, than a blade of grass. Of all the billions of people created, there is no one else who has ever lived or who is alive now that is just like you. You are a divine original.

Sam is fifty-six years of age, and throughout his life he has hated himself. Sometimes mildly, sometimes severely. Why? Listen as he sits in his pastor's study and pours out his story. "All my life," Sam said, "I have tried to be somebody else and I've been miserable. I never dared to be myself. I didn't think I was good enough, so I've been a phony for over half a century." That's the trouble with so many of us, we're always trying to be someone else and that's impossible: God never intended for you to be another person. He made you to be yourself. Do yourself a favor, be yourself.

Accept this fact: You are not inferior to anyone. Different, yes, wonderfully different. Wouldn't it be a dull world if we were all just alike? Never forget that you are God's idea—and God only dreams up fantastic ideas.

One of the worst crimes you can commit against yourself is to play the Comparison Game. Don't do it—don't compare yourself with another person. It is not God's best for you; it is an unhealthy thing

14

to do. We need to get it through our heads that we were never made to be like any other person. Accept yourself for who you are, and with God's help become that wonderful person he created you to be. Refuse to play the Comparison Game and be a healthier, happier person.

God loves you!

The boy who held his little boat and said, "It's mine, I made it," suffered a keen disappointment. One day, with exuberant anticipation, he carried his boat to the shore of the lake and sailed it on the clear, blue water. The little boat skimmed along as the gentle breeze blew its sails across the rippling waves. Then suddenly, a gust of wind caught the little boat and snapped the string the boy was holding. Out farther and farther the little boat sailed until at last it had vanished from sight. Sadly the boy made his way home—without his prized possession. It was lost.

The weeks and the months went by. Then one day as the boy passed a toy shop, something caught his attention. Could it be? Was it really? He looked closer. It was. Yes, there in the display window was his own little boat. Overjoyed, the boy bolted into the store and told the owner about the boat on display. It really belonged to him. He had made it, hadn't he? "I'm sorry," the shopkeeper said, "but it's my boat now. If you want it, you'll have to pay the price for it."

Sad at heart, the boy left the store. But he was determined to get his boat back, even though it meant working and saving until he had enough money to pay for it.

15

At last the day came. Clutching his money in his fist, he walked into the shop and spread his hard-earned money on the counter top. "I've come back to buy my boat," the boy said. The clerk counted the money. It was enough. Reaching into the showcase, the storekeeper took the boat and handed it to the eager boy. The lad's face lit up with a smile of satisfaction as he held the little boat in his arms. "You're mine," he said, "twice mine. Mine because I made you, and now, mine because I bought you."

Not only did God make you, but in Christ he paid the price to buy you back. Why? Because God believes you are worth loving.

Two birds were flying through the morning breeze, when one said to the other, "Look down at all those humans fretting." To this the other bird replied, "You know, they must not have a Heavenly Father like you and me." Jesus said, "Look at the birds! They don't worry about what to eat—they don't need to sow or reap or store up food—for your heavenly Father feeds them. And you are far more valuable to him than they are" (Matthew 6:26).

God believes you are worth saving. "You mean even with my sins?" Yes! "Even with that which is degrading to look at about myself?" Yes! "With all my faults?" Yes! "With all my shameful past?" Yes! God looks beyond everything that is wrong with us and sees the good, the great potential. God sent Jesus Christ to die on a cross to eliminate the bad, the degrading, the shameful—our sin—and to bring out the best in us. God believes in you. Jesus Christ died to restore your lost self-respect. To give you back dignity. To make you able to walk with

16

your head up high. Wow! What a great love God has for you.

Make this glorious realization yours: *"God loves me."* When Karl Barth, one of the great theologians of this century, came to America in 1960 to lecture at a seminary in Chicago, people came from all over America to hear him. Just before the opening session in Chicago, a reporter asked Karl Barth, "Mr. Barth, what is the most profound thought you have ever had?" Without a moment's hesitation, Karl Barth answered, "The most profound thought I know is the one expressed in a children's song my mother taught me as a boy—'Jesus loves me, this I know, 'cause the Bible tells me so!' " What could be greater than to be loved by God?

God loves you. Who are you to not love what God loves?

Three times during the last several months, Harriet had tried to take her own life. A friend had brought her to my office in desperation over her threats to do herself in. As I looked at Harriet, I saw the face of a depressed person who thought she had nothing to live for. She felt worthless, useless, unloved.

She talked for a long time. Then I said, "Now I've listened to you, will you listen to me for just a few moments?" She agreed. I looked into her face and said, "Harriet, God loves you. He's got something better for you than this." And when she looked like she didn't believe me, I continued. I told her about Jesus and what he did when he died on a cross for her, how he proved God's love for her.

17

I said, "I want you to do something for me, I want you to say three words." She said, "It depends what they are." I said, "They're not hard to say, they're healing words. They're words that can change your self-condemnation to self-acceptance. Here they are: God loves me."

Resisting a little, she slowly said the three words. I said, "Say them again." Much easier this time, she said, "God loves me." I asked her to say them a third time and as she did, she smiled a little. She said, "This seems kind of silly." I said, "You want to have help, don't you, Harriet?" She said, "Yes, I need help." "Then make me this promise. For the next two days, every time you start to be depressed, I want you to say these three words: God loves me. Over and over again. Will you do that?" She promised me that she would.

Two days later Harriet called me on the phone, with some newfound excitement in her voice, and she said, "Pastor, it really works. God does love me! I feel like I have something to live for, I'm a loved person."

There is nothing more healing than to accept God's love.

To you, God says:

My child, I love you.
My child, I accept you.
My child, I care about you.
My child, I forgive you.
My child, I'm going to use you.
My child, I am with you all the way.
So now, accept God's love and love yourself.

18

To love yourself is the Christian thing to do!

To become like Jesus is to love what he loves—and he loves you.

Some people have the mistaken notion that it's wrong to have good feelings about oneself. How wrong they are! The truth is: It is a sin not to love what God loves. To love yourself is:

Not only the healthy thing to do,
Not only the decent thing to do,
Not only the way to be liberated from negative attitudes,
Not only freeing you to love others,
Not only respecting what God respects,
But—to love yourself is to do what Jesus told you to do.

He said: "Thou shalt love thy neighbor as *thyself*." During a time when my self-image was really suffering, I picked up Dr. Robert Schuller's book *Move Ahead with Possibility Thinking*, which I had read several times. My eyes fell on these lifting words: "I'm really a wonderful person when Christ lives in me. I've been too self-critical. I've been my own worst enemy. I'm a child of God. God loves me. I can do all things through Christ who strengthens me."[2]

As I finished reading these wonderful words, I bowed my head and said, "Thank you, Jesus, because you love me. I am a child of God." In those moments, a great sense of newness and a sense of

[2]Robert Schuller, *Move Ahead with Possibility Thinking* (Garden City, N.Y.: Doubleday & Co., Inc., 1967), p. 35.

being a worthwhile person, loved by God, flooded my mind. You, too, can let God give your self-image a new charge.

Only a worm was made to crawl and stay down. Stand up and become God's man, God's woman—love yourself.

Who am I? I am the greatest person anyone could ever be—not because I am perfect, but because I am a child of God! The Bible says, "As many as received him, to them gave he power to become the sons of God, even to them that believe on his name" (John 1:12). The minute one receives Jesus Christ as Lord and Savior, he is immediately adopted into the family of God. Right then Jesus gives that person the name Christian, with a lifetime to grow into that name. There is no one reading this book who can't become a child of God this moment. Open your heart's door, let Jesus come in. If you are not a child of God, it is for only one reason. You haven't yet accepted your rightful sonship that Jesus came to give you. Every child of God belongs to the royal family.

What could be greater than to be a child of God? Thank you, Jesus—I am your child.

In ancient architecture, there was no building that excelled the breathtaking splendor of the Temple which Solomon built for God. It was magnificent! It has been estimated, based on present-day construction costs, that it would cost more than the debt of World War II to build. Nothing was spared in its construction.

20

In the Old Testament, a great to-do was made over the building of the Temple in Jerusalem. Its magnitude and magnificence has not often been matched in history. It was the Holy Place where God's presence dwelt. Unbelievable, yet true, is this fact! Now, since Jesus has come, we are to be the "temples of God" (1 Corinthians 3:16). Think of it! You are to be the "temple of God." The living, breathing being in which God dwells.

At an early age I was taught that being the "temple of God" meant there were things I should not do to my body. This is true. However, in recent years I have discovered an even greater truth about what it means to be the "temple of God." If I am the temple of God, where God dwells, then I am even more magnificent and of far more beauty than the great Temple Solomon built. *Yes, you were created for something great—to be the temple of God* (1 Corinthians 6:19).

Created to be the temple of God—that's you!

I entered a house where there was little or no furniture, some boxes sitting around, books of pornography on the floor. There for the first time I met Darrel, who had just tried to commit suicide two days before and was on the verge of another attempt. He said, "I am worthless, I do not deserve to live." I looked into the face of a broken man, into eyes filled with pain and said, "My friend, God created you for something better than this." I shared with him the exciting truth of how he was to be the temple of God.

Six months later in a Pastor's Class, the same

Darrel prayed this prayer: "I thank you, God, that I am your temple, because you love me and think I'm a worthwhile person. I now want to live. I am learning for the first time to love myself. Thank you, Jesus! Amen."

Not perfect—but becoming. So many people suffer from a sense of unworthiness because their lives do not measure up to their ideals. The emotional cost of being unwilling to accept anything unless it is perfect is very high. If you have strong tendencies toward being a perfectionist, you need to admit it. Then you need to accept the fact that no one except Jesus Christ himself has ever been perfect in performance. Having the love of God in life is not conditional upon your doing everything perfectly. You don't have to prove anything to God, he accepts you as you are. He says to you, "Let's go from here to become the wonderful person I created you to be."

Dr. Allen, pastor of one of the largest Methodist churches in the world, tells this story: "An outcast beggar was sitting across the street from an artist's studio. The artist saw him and quickly began to paint his portrait. When it was finished, he called the beggar over to look at it. At first the beggar did not recognize himself. 'Who is it?' he kept asking. The artist smiled and said nothing. The beggar kept looking at the portrait until recognition began to dawn. Hesitantly he asked, 'Is it me? Can it be me?' The artist replied, 'That is the man I see in you.' Then the beggar made a wonderful reply, 'If that's the man you see, that's the man I'll be.' "[3]

[3]Charles L. Allen, *Life More Abundant* (Old Tappan, N.J.: Fleming H. Revell Company). Used by permission.

You can become that beautiful person God created you to be.

You are to be used of God to do wonderful things. Jesus said: "You're the salt of the earth . . . the light of the world." Life for you is not over, you are not washed up, you are not too old. You have not made too many mistakes.

David committed the sins of adultery, murder and cover-up. When he repented and came clean with God, God loved him and used him. God will use you. Believe it!

There is no greater thing than to be used of God.

CHOOSE AND CULTIVATE A POSITIVE ATTITUDE

A man with a positive attitude may be knocked down, but never beaten. Many will say there is no way, but a man with a positive attitude will always find a way. Multitudes of people never achieve because they give up. The positive man is a high achiever because he never gives up. The positive person, whether he knows our Achiever's Creed or not, lives by it. Based on Philippians 4:13, here it is:

Whatever the mind can conceive
and I will dare to believe,
with God's help, I can achieve.

Next to knowing Jesus Christ personally as Lord and Savior, there is nothing more important than having a positive mental attitude. Your attitude can:

Make you or break you.
Heal you or hurt you.
Make you friends or make you enemies.
Put you uptight or put you at ease.
Make you miserable or make you happy.
Make you a failure or make you an achiever.

Some people today think the whole world stinks. Once a cranky grandpa lay down to take a nap. To have a little fun, his grandson put some limburger cheese on his mustache under his nose. Grandpa awoke with a snort, charged out of the bedroom and shouted, "This room stinks!" On through the house he went, shouting louder, "This whole house stinks!" He charged out on the porch and shouted as loud as he could, "The whole world stinks!" The truth is, it was Grandpa who stunk. The problem was under his own nose. Ninety-nine times out of 100, when we begin to feel like things stink, the problem is not with the world or with others, but ourselves. Our own attitudes have become negative. Change negative attitudes to positive ones, and you change your world.

To live in a better world, become a positive thinker.

Henry J. Kaiser tells this personal story about one time when he was building a levee along a river bank. There came a great storm and flood which buried all of his earth-moving machinery and destroyed the work that had been done. Upon going out to observe the damage after the water receded, he found his workers standing around glumly looking at the mud and the buried machinery.

He came among them and said with a smile, "Why are you so glum?"

"Don't you see what has happened?" they asked. "Our machinery is covered with mud."

[4]Charlie "Tremendous" Jones, *Life Is Tremendous*, (Wheaton, Ill.: Tyndale House Publishers, 1968), p. 13. Used by permission.

"What mud?" he asked brightly.

"What mud!" they repeated in astonishment. "Look around you. It is a sea of mud."

"Oh," he laughed, "I don't see any mud."

"But how can you say that?" they asked him.

"Because," said Mr. Kaiser, "I am looking at a clear blue sky, and there is no mud up there. There is only sunshine, and I never saw any mud that could stand against sunshine. Soon it will be dried up, and then you will be able to move your machinery and start all over again." What makes the difference between seeing mud and seeing sunshine? The difference is in attitude.

In the final analysis, it is your own attitude that will make you or break you, not what has happened to you.

The power to choose your attitude is yours.

Without a doubt, the human mind is the most awe-inspiring creation of God. The mind of man would stand above all the other miracles of Creation if they were listed in an order of importance. What you can do with your mind is really fantastic. Within it you have a will, the ability to reason, the feelings of emotions, the ability to reach beyond with your imagination, the inner conscience, the five physical senses, the recorder of memory, the sixth sense, and the subconscious. When one thinks about the human mind that the Master Creator has created for us, he has to stand in utter amazement.

Exercise mind control.

27

Who controls your mind? You do! Your mind is the one thing over which the Creator has given you complete control. God, himself, will not set this aside or reverse it, or do anything to change it. To you, God has given the right and the ability to control your own mind.

At one low point in my life when each day was a fight for survival, I came across the story of Dr. Victor Frankl. As this courageous man stood under the glaring lights of the Gestapo court in a Nazi concentration camp, soldiers took from him every earthly possession—his clothes, watch, even his wedding ring. Dr. Frankl said that as he stood there naked, his body shaved, he was destitute but for one thing. It was something that no one could take away from him. He realized in that moment that he still had the power to choose his own attitude. In my broken situation a lot of things were out of my control. For a controlled person like myself, this was most difficult. But the one thing I still had was the power to choose my own attitudes.

No matter what happens the attitude choice is still yours.

I am not responsible for anyone's attitudes and actions but my own. What an important principle this is! Especially is this important for all those who are now hurting from what they feel someone else has done or is doing. Hundreds of times in my journey from brokenness to wholeness I had to remind myself of this truth. I am responsible for no one else's attitudes and actions, but I am responsible to God for my own attitudes and actions. I discovered that when my own attitudes and actions were right, I could live with myself and enjoy good feelings toward others.

No shattering experience leaves one where it found him. It is the attitude that determines where the emotional heartbreak will leave him. By the choice of your own attitude, your heartbreak can remain with you or you can leave it behind. "Life," someone said, "is 10 percent what happens to you, and 90 percent how you react to what happens to you." No matter what happens to you, choose positive thoughts and sooner or later, you will be the winner. On the other hand, if you give in to negative thoughts, allowing them to dwell within your mind, there is no way that you will be anything but the loser.

Your attitude is far more important than anything else.

Your attitude is more important than:

Facts
Circumstances
What others say
Your past
Your education
Money

Dr. Samuel Shoemaker tells the delightful story of an elderly woman who was knocked down by a tire that flew off a passing truck. The accident left her with a broken hip and confined her to a small room for the rest of her days. There is always the chance that one will grow bitter, or at least become impatient with such circumstances. Not that lovely lady! When Dr. Shoemaker stood by her in the hospital, she looked up from her bed of intense pain and, with a wonderful smile, said, "Well, I wonder what God has for me to do here." What a beautiful, positive attitude.

When trouble bowls you over, when you are at the bottom emotionally, it's still a matter of choice. No one else can decide for you. You alone must choose whether you'll let trouble lick you, or whether you'll take courage and, with God's help, lick the trouble. There is nothing in this world that can happen to you but what, with God's help, and with a positive attitude, you can come out on top.

Created to be the master over circumstances, not to be mastered by them—that's you!

My close friend Tom Burton is mastering some very difficult circumstances with a persistent positive attitude. Two years ago Tom owned three survey companies in the State of Oregon, and one construction company. At that time he had more than one hundred people working for him. However, through a chain of reverses, Tom found himself having more in liabilities against his companies than he had assets. For two years he went through the grueling, painful process of winding all the businesses down, trying to satisfy all the creditors when there wasn't enough money to even begin to go around. He was being harassed and hammered by multitudes of people demanding payment, and for the first time did not know where the next paycheck was going to come from to provide for his family. Talk about going through deep, troubled waters! He and his family have been through it.

During those many months I never heard my friend even once say any word to even imply that he was beaten. Instead, I heard him say, "We'll make it, we'll put the past behind us." "I'll get it going again." "When I build it the next time, it will be better, and I won't make all the mistakes I made in the past." Tom is making it, and he's going to make it bigger and better than it ever was before. I can predict this because Tom has two of life's most worthwhile ingredients:

1. He has the wisdom to learn from all his experiences.

2. He has a positive attitude that will not quit. Tom believes that, with Christ's help, he can do anything. With Christ's help you, too, can overcome.

Attitude is more important than fact.

Twelve Ways you can eliminate the negative and activate the positive.

To get out of the slump, to get over the hurdle, to get up and get going again, you've got to do something. A positive attitude isn't something that will just come to you automatically. Neither will it come to you by just living defensively. You must go on the offensive—do something—act! Here is what you can do to become that more positive person that you want to be.

1. Become an ambassador of good words to every person you meet every day. During the gas crisis in the winter of 1974, I drove into our neighborhood

31

service station. At that time around the gas stations, everyone's nerves were on edge because of long lines and not being able to buy gas when they wanted it. Many of the attendants became the object of the public's frustrations. Having waited a long time in line, I finally got up to the gas pump. The young man there gave me a big smile and said, "Hello, how are you today?" In spite of some trying circumstances, he had determined to spread good cheer and friendliness to everyone. He really gave me a lift. Now each time I go back to that station, and he is there, I am especially friendly and cheerful to him. Jesus taught that if we give, we will receive. That attendant gave to me, and he has received back many cheerful hellos. To fill your life with joy, give cheerful words to everyone you meet.

2. *No matter what happens, look for the good and you'll find it.* A positive thinker does not refuse to recognize the negative, he refuses to dwell on it. Positive thinking is a form of thought which habitually looks for the best results from the worst conditions. It is always possible to look for something good; to expect the best for yourself even though things look bad. And the remarkable fact is that when you seek good, you will find it.

This past spring my friend Pat Fettig walked through the "valley of the shadow of death." His twenty-four-year-old brother, Freddie, drowned in the Sandy River on a Sunday afternoon. For three long days Pat and others searched up and down the rugged rapids of the Sandy River looking for the body. A chain of prayer was put into action at New

Hope on Wednesday. Thursday morning I was there when the divers pulled the body out. As we were riding back to town, after having been through the ordeal of a lifetime, he looked at me and with a big, positive smile, he said, "Praise God, we found him. Thank you, Jesus!" Refuse to dwell on the negative. In every happening, look for the good.

Mary was an attractive woman in her early thirties who had been active in her church. She came to see me in my office to tell me she had had it with her husband. This very day she was going to see a lawyer and file for divorce against Frank. Surprised, I asked her to sit down and tell me about it. For the next hour I listened to a story about a monster, her husband. By the time she got finished I, too, thought it was all over. I felt sorry for the poor lady putting up with all this mistreatment. To myself, I thought, "Frank doesn't deserve a fine woman like Mary for his wife." However, my better judgment prevailed and I handed Mary a paper on which to draw. "Mary," I said, "I want you to draw a circle. Now put one black dot in there for everything that is wrong with your husband, Frank." I could tell she was really enjoying putting the dots in the circle. When she finally could not think of anything else, I said, "Mary, tell me what you see in that circle."

"Oh, a bunch of dirty old dots," she said.

"Mary, tell me what else you see."

"Just black dots, lots of them," she answered.

"Mary, how much of the total space in the circle is taken up by the dots? I want you to look at that other space, lots and lots of it, in comparison to the space taken up by the dots. Mary, before you go to see the lawyer, tell me about all the other, I mean all of Frank's good points."

At first it was hard for her to get started. But it got easier and easier as she shared Frank's good points. A miracle happened; her whole attitude changed, and to this day she is still married to Frank. Take the bigger look and see all the good.

3. *By an act of your will, fill your mind with what is positive.* The Bible tells us how to do it. Philippians 4:8—"Fix your thoughts on what is true and good and right. Think about things that are pure and lovely, and dwell on the fine, good things in others. Think about all you can praise God for and be glad about" (TLB).

One of the greatest builders of positive attitudes given in the Bible is also one of the hardest to swallow. Here it is: "In everything give thanks: for this is the will of God in Christ Jesus concerning you" (1 Thessalonians 5:18).

When are we to give thanks?

In suffering? Yes.
When treated unfairly? Yes.
When misunderstood? Yes.
When taken advantage of? Yes.
When things go well? Yes.
When things go wrong? Yes.

Give thanks in everything.

The Apostle Paul knew what he wrote about when he said, "Giving thanks always for all things unto God" (Ephesians 5:20). The Apostle's mission to Philippi was a big failure. Instead of being followed by eager listeners, Paul and his co-workers were seized, beaten, and thrown into a musty jail, where their feet were made fast in the stocks. There, instead of whining and complaining and looking on the dark side, they sang and gave thanks to God. Their thanksgiving was no more dependent on outward circumstances than was that of Jesus when on the same night he was betrayed, he took bread and gave thanks.

I have witnessed the most exciting, miraculous things in people's lives when they have really practiced this principle of giving thanks in everything. Dare to give thanks in everything and you, too, will see miracles.

All sunshine and no rain makes a desert.

1. *Never surrender to negative emotions.* When you feel the mighty onrush of a negative emotion, how do you handle it? Admit it, face it, but don't give in to it. A sure way to fight weeds is to plant thick, healthy grass. The way to destroy a negative emotion is to verbalize a positive statement. You counterattack the invading negative emotion by shooting the positive counterpart. How? By using an affirmation that will release the positive emotion. For instance, you feel bad because you can't quit smoking. You don't verbalize it negatively: "I wish I could quit smoking." By saying this you surrender to, and are overpowered by, this negative force. Instead say, "I enjoy not smoking." "I love the feeling of being free from an enslaving habit." "I love the clean taste in my mouth since I have

35

stopped smoking." By uttering these positive words, you have started stopping.

5. Practice the principle of replacement. For every negative emotion there's a positive emotion that can be selected by you to eliminate the negative one. Replace:

Anger with love,
Fear with faith,
Despair with hope,
Greed with generosity,
Sorrow with joy,
Complaint with gratitude,
Worry with trust,
Guilt with forgiveness.

6. Bar the suggestive, the lewd, the perverted, the immoral, and the vulgar from your mind. You can't feed on garbage and stay healthy and sound in mind. The Bible warns us: "Don't let the world squeeze you into its mold" (Romans 12:2, *Phillips*). "Be ye transformed by the renewing of your mind" (Romans 12:2, KJV). How do we keep our minds healthy and clean? By living in fellowship with God —living God's way instead of the way of the world.

Put garbage into your mind—you're going to get garbage out. Put good thoughts into your mind—and good actions will come out.

7. See good in others. We all know people who create a negative atmosphere wherever they go. Why? Because they like to talk about everything and everyone in a negative way. Watch this—see if it is

36

not true. Every time you talk negatively about another human being, you infect the atmosphere with bad feelings.

Years ago I knew a pastor who had something good to say about everyone. This man, although not highly educated for his calling, was a tremendous success; everyone loved him. Who wouldn't love such a positive person? Look for the good in everybody you meet and you will find it.

8. *Determine to take an attitude of love and goodwill toward others.* There is nothing uglier than a bad attitude. Like the pollution from a paper mill on a windy day, it makes everything stink. On the other hand there is nothing more beautiful than a good attitude toward other people. A good attitude will win you friends and influence people. A long time after issues are forgotten, people will remember you for your attitude, be it good or bad.

Change your attitude toward other people and other people will change their attitude toward you. Your attitude toward the people who are around you is always bound to transmit and communicate itself. They say that a dog knows when you do not like him. Well, if a dog knows when you do not like him, will not a human being, who is far more aware, sense your true feelings?

Essentially, getting people to like you is merely the other side of liking them. One of the very popular men of our century was the late Will Rogers. One of the statements that he made immortal was this: "I never met a man I didn't like." That may have been a slight fib, but I am sure Will Rogers did not regard it as such. That is the way people who knew him tell us he felt about people, and in return, people everywhere loved Will Rogers. Love people and they will love you back.

9. *Express appreciation and warm feelings to others.* Ninety-nine percent of the time, when bad thoughts are holding good thoughts out of our minds, it is because they are selfish thoughts. A common need of us all is to get our minds off ourselves.

The way to get your mind off yourself is to give yourself away. You can do this by expressing gratitude or words of appreciation, or showing love for another person. One of the most healing therapies in the world is to give oneself in friendship and service to another person.

It's a healthy thing to give yourself away.

10. *Practice positive prayer.* Several weeks ago on a Monday morning, two different people within an hour shared with me how they found themselves in a real state of confusion over the weekend due to happenings in their lives. But when they really got alone with God and poured it all out to him, there came peace within and ability to think clearly.

Nothing clears the mind like prayer.

The Bible has a lot to teach about how we can pray and anticipate a good outcome. Mark 11:24 (TLB) says, "You can pray for *anything*, and *if you believe, you have it*; it's yours." That is a tremendous offer! Just think. Whatever you ask and pray for, if

38

you believe that you receive it, you shall have it. And Mark 11:23 (TLB) says, "All that's required is that you really believe and have no doubt."

To practice believing is of primary importance. It is the winning force in any and all achievements. When you expect the best, you release a magnetic force in your mind which by a law of attraction tends to bring the best to you. But if you expect the worst, you release from your mind the power of repulsion which tends to force the best from you. It is absolutely amazing how believing the best can happily set in motion the powerful forces that make the best happen.

As you pray, fill your mind with these verses:

"If God be for us, who can he against us?" (Romans 8:31).

"They that wait upon the Lord shall renew their strength" (Isaiah 40:31).

"According to your faith be it unto you" (Matthew 9:29).

"I can do all things through Christ which strengtheneth me" (Philippians 4:13).

11. *You can count on it. God is good, and he has a plan for your life.* He will not fail you; he will not let you down. He will bring good out of bad. When Peter Marshall died, a prophetic voice was silenced at the age of 46. Catherine Marshall wrote: "On that chilly, January morning, 1949, as I looked at my husband's face for the last time, then turned to leave the bare little hospital room, it seemed like whistling in the dark to believe that God could bring good out of such tragic loss." But because of

39

it, Catherine Marshall has found a capacity to write in a way that has ministered to multitudes of people in their needs.

When I find my enthusiasm level dropping below the high energy standard I have set for myself, I can usually pinpoint the trouble—"I am not expecting anything much to happen today!" The solution is simple. Plan something big! Get an exciting idea and put it into action. It is so much fun to live expectantly.

12. Affirm these positive affirmations aloud:

God is stronger than the strongest.
God is my source.
God has a plan for my life.
God will bring good out of this bad situation.
God forgives me.
God is with me.
Nothing is impossible with God.

Expect the best—and you will get it.

Jesus Christ is the great attitude transformer. For the greatest change in attitude, come to know Jesus Christ as personal Lord and Savior. Sheryl Dintelman, a sixteen-year-old, is a different girl now than when she started at our drive-in church not quite two years ago. Her attitudes have been so transformed that she no longer looks to be a sad person but a happy, smiling person. Here is her testimony in a letter that I received a couple of days ago:

I love New Hope and all of its members so much. In fact, I've built the best part of my life on its very foun-

dation. Through New Hope God has answered my questions about life.

Sure, I have problems tangled up with the delicate threads of my future. But you see, God already has all of that under control and I can be at peace with myself in knowing that.

If I had only known that joy would replace sadness, that confidence would be planted in place of fear, and love sown instead of suspicion, I would have given my life to Jesus Christ long before I did. But you see, that was the whole problem. I didn't know Jesus and therefore, I couldn't have known.

God has really changed my life. I guess I expected him to just "zap" my life into changing like I could snap my fingers. It didn't happen that way, though. It happened gradually, slowly—slowly enough that I had the joy of experiencing that change that God wanted me to make.

I just realized one day that I was happier, more grateful than I could ever remember being since I was a little girl. The storm and lightning last night gave me a real feeling of closeness to God. I kept thinking of how small I felt next to that great Presence, like a little girl next to her father. I just knew that I didn't have to be afraid, that everything was under control. I knew then that nothing happens unless God wants it to happen. I kept thinking of the words "I made you and I will take care of you." The world really isn't that spooky when you know that God is bigger, is it? God bless.

Sincerely,
Sheryl Dintelman

Keep on keeping on. It takes not just one choice or two choices or three, but thousands of choices to become a positive-thinking person. Old habits do not die easily. New habits are established by great effort and persistence.

How do you eat an elephant? One bite at a time. How do you climb a ladder? A rung at a time. How do you cut down a tree? A chop at a time. How do you become a positive person? A choice at a time.

Keep keeping on, choosing positive thoughts.

Like attracts like. Think positive thoughts and you send out positive vibrations; you activate the positive world around you. You gather friends who are positive thinkers. These friends will cause you to think more postively, and you will become a more positive person. Think positively and you'll get positive results.

A man becomes what he thinks. The Bible says, "For as he thinketh in his heart, so is he" (Proverbs 23:7). One of my very favorite pieces of literature is *The Great Stone Face* by Nathaniel Hawthorne. On the side of the mountain was the face. It was strong, kind, and honorable. Living nearby was a boy by the name of Ernest. Day by day he would look at that face, and he was thrilled by what he saw. Through his boyhood and even after he became a man, Ernest spent many hours gazing upon the face on the mountain.

There was a legend that some day a man would appear in the community who would look exactly like the face. For years that legend had persisted. One day, when the people were discussing the legend, someone suddenly cried out, "Behold, behold, Ernest is himself the likeness of the Great Stone Face." Indeed, he was. He had become like his thoughts. So you will become like your thoughts.

"Your attitude should be the kind that was shown us by Jesus Christ" (Philippians 2:5, TLB).

A Christian friend of mine, Jerry Schmidt, works as a salesman for a newly formed sausage company. Recently, after work one night, the government inspector stopped Jerry and asked him why he was always so happy. Jerry smiled and said, "I'd be glad to tell you. I'm happy because Jesus Christ lives within me and is my personal Lord and Savior." The man smiled and said, "I thought so. Your attitude shows it."

What could be greater than to have the mind of Christ within? You, too, can have Christ's attitude within you.

○ ○ ○

BELIEVE THE BEST IS YET TO COME

The most fantastic things happen to people who believe. No less of an authority than Jesus Christ himself says you do not have to be defeated. You can overcome illness, you can overcome weakness, you can overcome sin, you can overcome heartbreak, you can overcome failure. There is nothing or no situation you cannot overcome if you will believe.

Belief can change what appears to be an impossible situation. Belief unlocks the door to power beyond our own imagination. All things are possible—only believe. Jesus said: "If thou canst believe, all things are possible to him that believeth" (Mark 9:23).

Belief is:

The magic that lights up one's life with possibilities.
The initiator of all achieving.
The hook-up to a power greater than we are.

Every one of us needs to be believed in. It is amazing what having someone believe in you does for your self-image! One day Andrew brought his brother Simon to Christ. Carefully the Lord sized him up. He saw in him certain weaknesses, but he

45

also saw possibilities. So Christ said to him, "Thou art Simon the son of Jona: thou shalt be called Cephas, which is by interpretation, A stone" (John 1:42). He was saying, "You are one thing now, but I see in you possibilities of being something else. I believe in you." We know at times the Lord's faith in Peter was severely tried, yet he kept on believing in him and eventually Peter became the man Jesus believed he could be.

A mother shared with me out of her broken heart concerning her son who was always in some kind of trouble. Time and time again this boy had broken his mother's heart. She came to me wanting to know what she could do to help her son get out of all the difficulty he was in. I said to her, "It looks to me like you have done everything a mother can do." Then I thought of the most important thing a mother could do for her son and added, "Just keep on believing in him." One of the greatest acts of love you can give to another person is to keep on believing in him, even when others have given up.

Jesus believes you are a dream that can come true. Someone has said that in the company of sinners Jesus dreamed of saints. To one who had missed the way he said, "Neither do I condemn thee, go and sin no more." Jesus did not minimize her sin, but neither did he fail to see her tremendous possibilities even as he saw her shameful past; he saw the possibilities of a new beginning and a better future, and this is what he chose to focus his attention on.

God believes in you, now believe in yourself.

All things are possible if you believe in God. Believing in the New Testament means receiving Jesus

Christ into your life as Savior and Lord. Everything good starts with a decision to believe Jesus Christ and invite him to come into your heart.

You want an unbeatable life? Believe in Jesus.
You want to be a child of God? Believe in Jesus.
You want to overcome defeat? Believe in Jesus.
You want to have a better life? Believe in Jesus.
You want to beat defeating selfishness? Believe in Jesus.
You want to eventually win? Believe and totally dedicate yourself to Jesus.

God has a plan for your life. Finding and following God's plan for your life is the soundest, surest way to self-confidence. There is no greater feeling than to be in right relationship with God. If you are not in right relationship, you can be—starting now.

Believe wholeheartedly in God—and for you life will become unbeatable. Make this the dominating thought of your mind—God and I together are undefeatable.

Throughout the morning I had been working very diligently in my study on this book. Noon came and so I decided to take a lunch break. As I came out of my office I heard Jim Bisel and my secretary talking in the next room. He had two of his six children with him. I could tell these two little girls loved their daddy very much by the special sparkle that was in their eyes. Jim's ministry is to make people happy. He does Christian entertainment in rest homes and hospitals. He had come to our office so he could use the mimeograph machine to run off a special sheet to be used in a promotional program with which he was working with one of the local business firms. Jim and I chatted together a little while, and as I started to walk out the door, before I knew it, Jim and his two little girls were singing a song for me, called "Side by Side," with great big smiles written all over their faces. Before I knew it, we were all laughing and enjoying ourselves.

As Jim was leaving, I walked on out to the door with him. Just before he went out the door he rather casually said, "By the way, you might pray a little special prayer for us this week. On Monday we had an accident and our car looks like an accordion; on Tuesday when I went to work I discovered I didn't have a job any more; on Wednesday the County Tax Department phoned to say we owed some taxes from four years back, and if we don't get these paid in ten days, they'll come out and auction off our home."

All the time Jim was telling about these enormous problems, he still had his warm friendly smile that glowed all over his face—so much so, it took a few minutes for me to respond to the fact he really had some pressing problems that I needed to help lift up in prayer.

My friend smiled again and said, "Have a good day, Pastor," and he was off to another nursing home where he and the girls were going to put on another program to make people happy. You see, Jim is a man who has faith, hope and love. If you ask him why he is happy, he would tell you it is Jesus Christ who inspires him to smile and laugh.

As a result his faith has now grown until no

matter what blow hits him, he has that overcoming power that just keeps on smiling and moving ahead.

With God's help you can get on top of anytng. "I can do all things through Christ which strengtheneth me" (Philippians 4:13).

Only believe! The word belief is symbolic of a power that has no limitations within reason, and we find evidence of its influence wherever we find people who have achieved success in any calling.

They conquer who believe they can.

A few months ago, the television was on in our home and my wife Margi was surprised to hear our Achiever's Creed over the evening news. Channel 8 here in Portland was doing a news story on a lady who is an employee at a bus company. Her job is to answer the phone all day and take people's complaints and complaints. Now this is one job I am sure I do not want—to have to listen to complaining people all day long. But because this lady had done such a great job of being warm and friendly in the midst of some pretty difficult conversations, the news had singled her out for honor in a news story. In the midst of the filmed conversation, the reporter asked her how she kept her cool with people who were usually upset. This charming lady simply pointed to New Hope's Achiever's Creed, hanging on her wall and read it aloud:

Whatever the mind can conceive
and I will dare to believe,
with God's help, I can achieve.

Faith in God can move a mighty mountain.

49

Never stop believing

Lay hold of the power to persevere. To achieve, to overcome, to win the prize, one must lay hold of the power to persevere. God's Word says, "Let us run with perseverance the race that is set before us" (Hebrews 12:1, RSV). Those who come out on top are those who stick with it through thick and thin.

The Bible constantly admonishes us to develop a steadfastness that is unmovable, always abounding and going forward toward the goal. There is no place for a quitter in the band of those who would live to win.

Quitters never win. Winners never quit.

History tells us the average speed of the Mayflower during the voyage across the Atlantic was just two miles per hour. That was slow enough to discourage even the most seasoned sailor, yet that voyage is remembered today as a glorious example of what persistence can achieve. There is almost nothing persistence cannot achieve in time.

Anything worthwhile is worth taking the time to achieve.

Be willing to take the time to achieve your goals. If you are like me, you are impatient. Allow yourself to get impatient and you get all tensed up. We must remind ourselves: Anything worthwhile takes a while. The more worthy a goal is, the longer you can afford to work at it before it is achieved. The question is: Is this a worthy project? If so, then "let us not be weary in well doing: for in due season we shall reap, if we faint not" (Galatians 6:9). In the Bible and written in the universe is "the undeniable law of sowing and reaping."

The greatest man who ever lived, who had the greatest mission to achieve, had to wait. Though Jesus was anxious to get started to see results, to make it happen, for thirty long years he waited before he began his public ministry.

Instead of being out preaching the good news of the Kingdom, he sawed planks and hammered nails in a carpenter shop. Such a menial task for the Son of God to be doing! But as one studies the life of Jesus, he's made to realize that all the waiting was a part of his important preparation. The opportunities of his limited "today" became the stones out of which he built his eternal kingdom tomorrow.

Waiting is a hard thing to do. We're all children of the instamatic age, the now generation. Waiting through the difficult times is God's way of preparing us for better things to come. James writes, "Dear brothers, is your life full of difficulties and temptations? Then be happy, for when the way is rough, your patience has a chance to grow. So let it grow, and don't try to squirm out of your problems. For when your patience is finally in full bloom, then you will be ready for anything, strong in character, full and complete" (James 1:2-4, TLB). What finer point is there to be developed in our Christ-like character than patience.

Patience is faith pushed to its farthest degree.

Are you facing a difficult time in your life? Don't stop believing, don't give up. Practice patience—know that time can make all the difference in your world. Somehow we must discover that time can be put to work for the good of those who love God, and learn to practice patience. Do this, and with the passing of months and years you will find solutions to seemingly impossible problems.

God's timing is perfect.

I have had absolutely miraculous answers to prayer in my personal life. There was the time when I had just finished college and was making the tragic mistake of taking the pastorate of a little struggling church instead of going on to seminary. Then a friend phoned unexpectedly from miles away and came and took me 700 miles to a convention in Kansas City.

As long as I live I will be grateful for what happened there. On a Sunday afternoon, having asked God to direct my future, I walked from the hotel to the convention hall where there were twenty thousand people. As I stepped in the front door I ran head-on into the president of the local seminary. Without even saying hello, he said, "Dale, I will see you in seminary in a few days." I said, "Yes, Lord," and packed up and went to seminary. God's timing was just right. The years have shown how crucial it was for me to attend seminary at that time in my life.

God has never promised to give us exactly what we asked for when we ask for it. Two years ago Margi and I had our house up for sale, preparing to use our resources to start New Hope. How impatient I became as the days passed so slowly without a sale—April, May, June, July, no sale. I thought, Where is God in all this? Then just at God's perfect timing it sold. Not a day too soon or a day too late. A few days later we left to attend Dr. Schuller's

Institute for Successful Church Leadership in Garden Grove, California. At the end of August, when we returned, the house deal closed immediately and we moved into an apartment in southeast Portland and launched the ministry of New Hope. As Dr. Schuller told us at the Institute: "God's delays are not God's denials."

Be patient—believe—God is working everything out.

No man is ever beaten until he loses his patience.

Great men just will not be stopped. My Grandfather Galloway was a man with that kind of determination. As I was growing up, Grandpa Galloway would come from Arizona to visit us in the summer time. On several occasions the camp meeting that my dad directed would be in progress. Invariably the people would ask for Grandpa to sing. Up in years, his voice would crack, and I am sure he would not win any music contests, but he would look up into the heavens and sing the favorite song he had written, and somehow when he sang, heaven came closer to earth. Appropriately enough the title of his own song was, "You Can't Stop Me." As I remember it, here's how Grandpa wrote it and sang it:

I have many precious loved ones who have gone on
    before,
They are resting and waiting for me there;
I'll be ready and watching when the summons comes,
And that beautiful city we will share.
You can't stop me, you can't stop me,
I hear the voices calling o'er the sea;
I'll make it to that city through Calvary;

I feel his cleansing power and you can't stop me.

O. V. Galloway.

You, too, can join the nonstoppers headed for greater things, reaching beyond to the heavens.

Believe and never give up.

The best is yet to come.
Always keep hope going.

Recently I heard someone say another person was hopeless. Something inside of me cried out, That's not right. To my mind the most profane word in the English language is not a four-letter word, but the word "hopeless." To say a person is hopeless, or a situation is hopeless, is a direct denial of the power of God. In Psalm 42:5, we read this powerful statement: "Hope thou in God."

No man can live long without hope. Psychiatrists have discovered no matter how deeply a person is depressed, no matter how despondent, if somehow they can inject a ray of hope in a person's mind, he will begin to recover. There was a time in my life where some people said, "There's no hope for him." They were talking about me. But because Jesus Christ is alive, I still held on to hope. I refused to believe them. And now I am the useful pastor of a great, growing church.

Many a person in our society today feels hopeless for one reason or another. Never before in the history of the world have people been so beaten psychologically. It is our unwavering belief that in

54

Jesus Christ we have hope that all failure, all sins are forgiven. Now that biblical word *hope* is not something you wish for or dream of, but it is the assurance of the fact that God keeps his word.

God promises us that if we confess our sins, he is faithful and just to forgive us our sins. Good news: No one has to be beaten down by his sins another day. If you are beaten by your sins, your failures, confess them all to God and he will forgive you of every wrongdoing. I have never yet met a person that is hopeless. If you are alive, there is hope— there is Jesus!

If I could give to a man only one thing, I would give him hope. The kind of hope the Psalmist wrote about when he said: "For in thee, O Lord, do I hope" (Psalm 38:15). Hope in God is the only firm basis for achieving worthwhile aspirations.

A man who has hope can never be defeated.

What a difference between believing God causes tragic things to happen, and believing God allows them to happen. I, for one, do not believe God causes tragedy to come into our lives. God is not the author of evil; Satan is. A loving God permits incidents to occur for our own development and character.

When they first manufactured golf balls, they made the covers smooth. A certain young man, who was having severe financial difficulties, loved to play golf. He did not let the fact that he had only one old, beat up golf ball, keep him from playing. The men he was playing golf with had new, smooth, shiny golf balls. As they played, it was discovered

55

Pete's ball got a lot more distance and went straighter than the smooth balls. Today all golf balls are manufactured with dimples all over the covers. With these rough spots, the ball goes further. So it is with life. It takes some rough spots in your life to make you go the farthest, to bring the best out in you.

A man who has hope knows that God will bring something good out of bad.

I know an inspiring man of great faith who owned a lumber mill. Two summers ago, it was my privilege to be given a personal tour of this fascinating operation by the head man himself. Afterward he shared his tremendous faith in God with me as he related this experience:

In 1965, his mill was completely wiped out by fire. Only twenty percent of it was insured. From all appearances everything he and his family had worked a lifetime to build was wiped out.

Just before the fire, another small mill he owned, which had not been doing very well, had been put up for sale. A few days after the fire in the large mill, the small mill was sold. He took the money from the sale and insurance money, worked with his crews day and night for eighty straight days, and completely rebuilt the mill. Before the fire, lumber prices were a minimum of $48.00 per 1,000, to break even. However, in building the new plant, with many innovations and the best up-to-date machinery, the cost of the operation was reduced greatly. Just as the mill was completed, the price of lumber dipped to an all-time low and stayed there for the next year. If he had been operating the old mill, he would have lost $120,000 a month. But since the new mill was in operation, he was able to weather the storm. The next year, lumber rose to an all-time high. With tears in his eyes, he praised God and testified to the fact his Heavenly Father was taking care of him all the time.

My friend believes Romans 8:28, "And we know that all things work together for good to them that love God, to them who are the called according to his purpose." Here is the secret of true optimism—no matter what happens, God reigns, and he is at work to bring out good from bad. For the Christian, the best is yet to come.

One of my church members and friends had been in the hospital more than a dozen times during the past year. He and his family had been through so much I wondered how they could take any more. Now he was back in the hospital again, on the critical list, in the intensive care, cardiac section.

The morning after I went to visit him, his wife phoned. She said, "What in the world did you say to Glenn?" I said, "Well, I don't know, why?" "Well, before you went to see him yesterday he was so depressed and despondent. After you left, he was cheerful, at peace, and told me that if anything happened and he didn't make it, it would be all right, not to grieve, he would be well taken care of. He had a smile on his face."

After his wife hung up, I remembered what I had said to Glenn. I had quoted a few great faith-hope verses from the Bible and told him about a recent miracle of healing. Then I did something I had never done before. I said, "Glenn, look at it this way. When you know the Lord, as you do, the best is yet to come. If God heals you, that's going to be a whole lot better and if he doesn't, then you are going to go to Heaven and what could be better?" So I looked my friend right in the face and said, "Glenn, for you, the best is yet to come." And in that moment, Christian hope came alive. Wow! What a difference hope makes.

Since starting New Hope Community Church two years ago, we have been looking for the piece of land where we will fulfil our dream for building Oregon's first walk-in/drive-in church. The seven men who serve on our Board of Directors and myself have spent many hours in formulating the requirements for the piece of property we will purchase. The ten-acre plus spot must have accessibility to major freeways and visibility to passing traffic, must excel in natural beauty, and must be within fifteen minutes by car of one hundred thousand people plus.

After months of diligent searching, researching, and viewing, we found what we believe to be a beautiful spot, with perfect access to all the city's freeway systems.

Having used our God-given minds, we concluded that this spot not only met all our requirements but excelled in every point. We bowed our heads to ask God to guide in our decision-making. Talk about faith—here's a group of eight men deciding on whether or not to buy a piece of property that costs over $100,000, when they don't have even the money for the down payment. As each one of the men was praying and seeking God's will in this, God gave me New Hope's promise. Here it is:

Behold, I have set before thee an open door, and no man can shut it (Revelation 3:8).

Believing, we all said yes. This would be a great thing for God; it would help a lot of hurting people; it would pull the very best out of all of us. Believing we claimed that marvelous scenic piece of property upon which to fulfil our God-given dream. You, too, have an open door before you.

To you God has given:

Healing for all your hurts.
Insights to build a better life.
Love to give away.
New dreams to dare you to reach beyond where you have been.
Obstacles to overcome.
Scars to turn into stars.

To you God has given: possibilities unlimited.
For you the sky is the limit. What matters is not where you have been—but where you are going.

Believe it—never stop believing, the best is yet to come!

◯ ◯ ◯